Financial Freedom for Women

Your Ultimate Guide to Money

Management and Independence

By

Samantha Grey

Table of Contents

Introduction

The Importance of Financial Independence for Women

Financial independence is a transformative goal that empowers women to take control of their lives, make informed decisions, and build a secure future. In a world where financial literacy is often overlooked in traditional education, gaining the knowledge and skills to manage your finances is crucial. This book aims to

provide practical guidance, actionable steps, and the confidence needed to achieve financial independence.

My Journey and Motivation for Writing This Book

Like many women, I faced numerous financial challenges throughout my life. From dealing with student loans and credit card debt to navigating career changes and unexpected expenses, I realised the importance of having a solid financial foundation.

My journey to financial independence was filled with learning experiences, and I am passionate about sharing these insights with you. This book is a culmination of my knowledge, research, and personal experiences, designed to help you avoid common pitfalls and achieve financial success.

What Readers Can Expect to Learn

Throughout this book, you will learn how to assess your current financial situation, set achievable goals, create

and stick to a budget, save effectively, manage debt, improve your credit score, invest wisely, plan for retirement, and explore entrepreneurship. Each chapter is packed with practical advice, real-life examples, and step-by-step guides to help you take control of your financial future.

Chapter 1

Understanding Financial Independence

Financial independence means having enough income to cover your living expenses without relying on employment or assistance. It's the freedom to make choices that are not influenced by financial constraints, whether that's pursuing a passion, starting a business, or simply enjoying a comfortable retirement. For women, financial independence is particularly significant as it promotes equality, reduces dependency, and provides a safety net in times of need.

Common Myths and Misconceptions

Myth 1: **Financial Independence is Only for the Wealthy**

Many believe that financial independence is an unattainable goal

unless you have a high income or inherit wealth. This is not true. Financial independence is achievable for anyone willing to plan, save, and invest wisely. It's about making smart financial decisions and living within your means.

Myth 2: **You Have to Be a Financial Expert**

You don't need to be a financial guru to achieve financial independence. While knowledge helps, the most critical aspect is discipline and

consistency. This book provides you with the essential knowledge, and with time, you will become more comfortable and confident in managing your finances.

Myth 3: **It's Too Late to Start**

Regardless of your age or financial situation, it's never too late to start

working towards financial independence. The key is to begin now. The earlier you start, the more time you have to grow your wealth, but even small steps taken later in life can lead to significant improvements in your financial health.

Benefits of Achieving Financial Independence

Empowerment and Confidence

Achieving financial independence boosts your confidence and empowers you to make choices that

align with your values and goals. It allows you to take control of your life and reduce the stress and anxiety associated with financial instability. Financial independence provides the freedom to pursue your passions and interests without being tied to a job for the sake of a paycheck. It gives you the flexibility to take risks, such as starting a business or taking a career break, without worrying about financial repercussions.

Having a solid financial foundation ensures that you are prepared for unexpected events such as job loss, medical emergencies, or economic downturns. Financial independence acts as a safety net, providing peace of mind and stability in uncertain times. With financial independence, you have the resources to invest in personal and professional growth.

Whether it's furthering your education, travelling, or exploring

new hobbies, financial stability opens up a world of opportunities. Financial independence reduces dependency on others, whether it's a partner, family members, or government assistance. It allows you to stand on your own and make decisions that are best for you and your future.

Understanding the true meaning and importance of financial independence is the first step on your journey.

Dispelling common myths and recognizing the numerous benefits can motivate and inspire you to take control of your finances. In the following chapters, we will delve into practical steps and strategies to help you achieve financial independence and build a secure and fulfilling future.

Chapter 2

Assessing Your Current Financial Situation

The first step towards financial independence is understanding where you stand financially. This involves a thorough evaluation of your income and expenses.

1. Calculate Your Income

- Primary Income:Include all sources of primary income such as salary, wages, bonuses, and business profits.

- Secondary Income: Account for secondary income like freelance work, side hustles, rental income, dividends, and any other sources.

2. Track Your Expenses
- Fixed Expenses:These are regular monthly expenses that remain constant, such as rent/mortgage, utilities, insurance premiums, loan payments, and subscriptions.

- Variable Expenses:These fluctuate monthly and include groceries, dining

out, entertainment, travel, and miscellaneous purchases.

3. Identify Patterns

Analyse your spending habits over the past few months. Identify areas where you tend to overspend and opportunities for savings. Tools like budgeting apps or spreadsheets can help you track and categorise expenses efficiently.

Understanding Your Net Worth

Your net worth provides a snapshot of your financial health by comparing what you own (assets) to what you owe (liabilities).

1. List Your Assets
- Cash and Cash Equivalents:Savings accounts, checking accounts, cash on hand.
- Investments: Stocks, bonds, mutual funds, retirement accounts.

- Property: Real estate, vehicles, valuable personal items (art, jewellery).
- Other Assets: Any other valuable items not previously mentioned.

2. List Your Liabilities
- Short-term Debt: Credit card balances, personal loans, unpaid bills.

- Long-term Debt: Mortgages, car loans, student loans, any other significant debts.

3. Calculate Net Worth

Subtract your total liabilities from your total assets to determine your net worth. This figure provides a clear picture of your financial position and helps you set realistic financial goals.

Identifying Financial Habits and Patterns

Reflect on your financial behaviour to understand the habits that influence your spending and saving. Consider the following questions:

- Do you often spend impulsively?
- Are there specific categories where you consistently overspend?
- How frequently do you review your financial status?
- Are you saving regularly, or do you save inconsistently?

Recognizing your financial habits is essential for making necessary adjustments and improving your overall financial health.

Chapter 3

Setting Financial Goals

Setting clear financial goals is crucial for achieving financial independence. These goals can be categorised into short-term and long-term.

1. Short-term Goals

These are goals you aim to achieve within a year or less. Examples include:

- Building an emergency fund
- Paying off a credit card balance
- Saving for a vacation
- Reducing monthly expenses

2. Long-term Goals

These goals extend beyond a year and often require more significant planning and saving. Examples include:

- Saving for retirement

- Buying a home

- Funding higher education

- Achieving complete financial independence

SMART Goals Framework

Using the SMART framework can help you set effective and achievable financial goals.

1. Specific

Clearly define what you want to achieve. For example, instead of saying "I want to save money,"

specify "I want to save $5,000 for an emergency fund."

2. Measurable

Establish criteria to measure your progress. For example, "I will save $400 per month to reach my $5,000 goal in 12 months."

3. Achievable

Ensure your goal is realistic based on your financial situation. Assess your

income and expenses to determine a feasible savings plan.

4. Relevant

Set goals that align with your broader financial objectives. Prioritise goals that contribute significantly to your financial independence.

5. Time-bound

Assign a timeline to your goal. For example, "I will save $5,000 for an emergency fund within 12 months."

Creating a Vision Board for Financial Success

A vision board is a powerful tool to visualise and stay motivated towards your financial goals. Here's how to create one:

1. Gather Supplies

Collect magazines, photos, quotes, and other materials that inspire you. You'll also need a board, scissors, glue, and markers.

2. Visualise Your Goals

Think about your financial goals and what achieving them looks like. Find images and words that represent these goals.

3. Assemble Your Board

Arrange and glue the images and words on the board. Group related goals together and add personal touches with drawings or handwritten notes.

4. Display Your Vision Board

Place your vision board where you'll see it daily. It serves as a constant reminder of your goals and keeps you focused and motivated.

Chapter 4

Budgeting Basics

Budgeting is a cornerstone of financial management. It helps you allocate resources effectively, ensures you live within your means, and facilitates savings and investment. A well-structured budget can prevent overspending, reduce financial stress, and help you achieve your financial goals.

Different Types of Budgets

1. Zero-based Budget

In a zero-based budget, every dollar is allocated to a specific purpose, ensuring that your income minus expenses equals zero. This method provides a high level of control over your finances.

2. Envelope Method

With the envelope method, you allocate cash to different spending

categories using physical envelopes. This technique is especially effective for managing variable expenses and preventing overspending.

3. 50/30/20 Budget

The 50/30/20 budget divides your income into three categories: 50% for needs, 30% for wants, and 20% for savings and debt repayment. This method provides a balanced approach to spending and saving.

Step-by-Step Guide to Creating a Budget

1. Determine Your Income
Calculate your total monthly income from all sources. Use your net income (after taxes) to ensure accuracy.

2. List Your Expenses

Categorise your expenses into fixed and variable. Use past bank statements and receipts to ensure completeness.

3. Allocate Your Income
Assign portions of your income to each expense category. Ensure that your total expenses do not exceed your total income.

4. Track Your Spending

Monitor your spending throughout the month to ensure you stay within your budget. Use budgeting apps or spreadsheets to simplify tracking.

5. Adjust as Necessary

Review your budget regularly and make adjustments as needed. Life circumstances change, and your budget should be flexible enough to adapt.

Practical Budgeting Tips

1. Prioritise Needs Over Wants
Ensure that essential expenses
(housing, utilities, groceries) are

covered before allocating money to
discretionary spending.

2. Automate Savings
Set up automatic transfers to your
savings account to ensure you save
consistently. Treat savings as a non-
negotiable expense.

3. Cut Unnecessary Expenses

Identify and eliminate non-essential expenses. Small changes, like making

Coffee at home or reducing dining out, can add up over time.

4. Use Cash for Discretionary Spending

Consider using cash for categories where you tend to overspend. Physical cash provides a tangible limit and can help curb impulse buying.

5. Revisit Your Budget Regularly

Regularly review and update your budget to reflect changes in income, expenses, and financial goals. Monthly reviews can help you stay on track and make necessary adjustments.

Chapter 5

Saving Strategies

An emergency fund is a crucial component of financial stability. It provides a safety net to cover unexpected expenses, such as medical emergencies, car repairs, or job loss, without derailing your financial goals.

Aim to save three to six months'
worth of living expenses. Start with a
smaller goal, like $1,000, and build

from there. Keep your emergency
fund in a high-yield savings account
that is easily accessible but separate
from your everyday checking
account. Set up automatic transfers to
your emergency fund to ensure
consistent contributions.
If you need to use your emergency
fund, prioritise replenishing it as soon
as possible. Adjust your budget to

allocate extra money towards
rebuilding your fund.

Different Saving Methods and Tools

There are various strategies and tools
to help you save effectively. Choose
the methods that best suit your
financial situation and goals.

1. Pay Yourself First
Treat savings as a priority by setting
aside a portion of your income before

spending on other expenses. This ensures that saving becomes a regular habit.

2. Use Savings Challenges
Savings challenges, like the 52-week challenge, where you save an increasing amount each week, can make saving fun and motivate you to stay consistent.

3. Take Advantage of Employer Benefits

Utilise employer-sponsored retirement plans, health savings accounts (HSAs), and other benefits

that offer tax advantages and employer matches.

4. Utilise Savings Apps
Use apps like Digit, Qapital, or Acorns that round up your purchases to the nearest dollar and save the difference or automate small, regular transfers to your savings account.

Tips for Maximising Your Savings

1. Reduce Unnecessary Expenses

Identify and cut non-essential expenses. Consider negotiating bills, cancelling unused subscriptions, and finding cheaper alternatives for regular purchases.

2. Increase Your Income
Look for opportunities to increase your income through side hustles,

freelance work, or negotiating a raise. Additional income can accelerate your savings goals.

3. Take Advantage of Cash Back and Rewards

Use credit cards with cash back or rewards programs for your regular expenses. Ensure you pay off the balance in full each month to avoid interest charges.

4. Save Windfalls

Deposit any unexpected money, such as tax refunds, bonuses, or gifts, directly into your savings account to

boost your savings without impacting your budget.

5. Set Clear Savings Goals
Having specific goals, like saving for a vacation, a down payment on a house, or an emergency fund, can motivate you to save more diligently.

Chapter 6

Managing Debt

(Good vs. Bad Debt)

Not all debt is created equal.

Understanding the difference between good and bad debt can help you make informed decisions about borrowing.

1. Good Debt

Mortgage Loans: Investing in property can build equity and provide long-term financial benefits.

Student Loans: Education can increase earning potential and provide a return on investment over time.

Business Loans: Borrowing to start or expand a business can lead to increased income and growth opportunities.

2. Bad Debt

Credit Card Debt: High-interest rates and revolving balances can lead to significant financial strain.

Payday Loans: These short-term loans often come with exorbitant interest rates and fees.

Consumer Loans: Borrowing for depreciating assets, like cars or electronics, can lead to financial loss over time.

Strategies for Paying Off Debt

1. Debt Snowball Method

This method focuses on paying off the smallest debt first while making minimum payments on other debts. Once the smallest debt is paid off, you move to the next smallest, creating a snowball effect.

2. Debt Avalanche Method

With this approach, you prioritise paying off the debt with the highest interest rate first while making minimum payments on the others.

This method can save you more money on interest over time.

3. Debt Consolidation

Consolidating multiple debts into a single loan with a lower interest rate can simplify payments and potentially reduce overall interest costs. Options include personal loans, balance transfer credit cards, or home equity loans.

4. Negotiating with Creditors

Contact your creditors to negotiate lower interest rates, reduced balances, or more favourable repayment terms. Many creditors are willing to work with you if you're proactive and communicative.

Debt Consolidation and Negotiation Tips

1. Understand Your Options

Research various consolidation options, including personal loans,

balance transfer cards, and home equity loans. Compare interest rates, fees, and repayment terms to find the best solution.

2. Create a Repayment Plan
Develop a clear plan to pay off your consolidated debt. Ensure that the new payment fits within your budget and that you're committed to paying it off as quickly as possible.

3. Seek Professional Help

If you're overwhelmed by debt, consider seeking help from a credit counselling agency. They can provide guidance, negotiate with creditors, and help you create a manageable repayment plan.

4. Stay Disciplined
Avoid accumulating new debt while paying off existing debt. Focus on

living within your means and sticking to your budget.

Chapter 7

Credit Scores and Reports

Your credit score is a critical factor that affects your ability to borrow money, rent an apartment, and even secure certain jobs. Understanding and maintaining a good credit score can save you money and open up financial opportunities.

1. Components of a Credit Score

Payment History (35%): Timely payments on loans and credit cards.

Credit Utilisation (30%):The ratio of your credit card balances to your credit limits.

Length of Credit History (15%):The age of your credit accounts.

New Credit (10%): Recent credit inquiries and newly opened accounts.

Credit Mix (10%): A variety of credit types, such as credit cards, mortgages, and auto loans.

2. Checking Your Credit Score

You can check your credit score for free through various online services or credit card companies. Regularly monitoring your score helps you stay informed and take action if needed.

How to Read a Credit Report

A credit report is a detailed record of your credit history. Reviewing your credit report regularly can help you identify and correct errors, detect fraud, and understand your credit

health. You're entitled to a free credit report from each of the three major credit bureaus (Equifax, Experian, and TransUnion) once a year. You can request your reports at AnnualCreditReport.com.

Check out the key Sections of a Credit Report:

- Personal Information: Name, address, social security number, and employment history.

- Credit Accounts: Details of all credit accounts, including the type of account, credit limit, balance, and payment history.
- Credit Inquiries: A record of companies that have checked your credit.

- Public Records: Information on bankruptcies, foreclosures, and other legal matters.
- Collections: Accounts sent to collections agencies for non-payment.

Review your credit report carefully for inaccuracies. If you find any errors, dispute them with the credit bureau. Provide documentation to support your claim, and follow up until the issue is resolved.

Tips for Improving and Maintaining a Good Credit Score

1. Pay Bills on Time

Timely payments are the most significant factor affecting your credit

score. Set up automatic payments or reminders to ensure you never miss a due date.

2. Keep Credit Utilisation Low

Aim to keep your credit card balances below 30% of your credit limits.

Paying off your balances in full each month is ideal.

3. Avoid Opening Too Many New Accounts

Multiple credit inquiries within a short period can negatively impact your credit score. Apply for new credit only when necessary.

4. Maintain a Mix of Credit Types

Having a mix of credit accounts (credit cards, instalment loans, mortgages) can positively affect your credit score. However, don't open new accounts just to diversify your credit mix.

5. Keep Old Accounts Open

The length of your credit history affects your score, so keeping older accounts open can be beneficial. Closing accounts can reduce your available credit and negatively impact your utilisation ratio.

6. Monitor Your Credit Regularly
Regularly check your credit reports and scores to stay informed about your credit status. Address any issues promptly to maintain a healthy credit profile.

Chapter 8

Investing 101

Investing is a powerful tool for building wealth and achieving financial independence. Understanding the fundamentals of investing can help you make informed decisions and grow your money over time.

Compound interest is the process where the money you earn from investments generates additional earnings. The longer your money remains invested, the more it can grow exponentially. Example: If you invest $1,000 at an annual return of 7%, it will grow to approximately $2,000 in 10 years and $4,000 in 20 years, illustrating the exponential growth potential of compound interest.

Investments come with varying levels of risk and return. Higher potential returns usually involve higher risk. Understanding your risk tolerance and investment time horizon is crucial for making suitable investment choices.

-Risk Tolerance: Your comfort level with the potential for losing money in the short term.

-Time Horizon: The length of time you plan to keep your money invested before needing to withdraw it.

Also, spreading your investments across different asset classes (stocks, bonds, real estate) to reduce risk. A well-diversified portfolio can help protect your investments from market volatility.

Different Types of Investments

1. Stocks : this includes shares of ownership in a company. Historically, stocks offer high returns but come

with higher volatility . Investing in individual stocks requires research and monitoring. Alternatively, you can invest in index funds or mutual funds for broad market exposure.

2. Bonds: Loans made to corporations or governments, which pay interest over time. Generally lower returns compared to stocks but with lower risk. Bonds can provide steady income and help balance a more aggressive investment portfolio.

3. Mutual Funds: Pooled funds from multiple investors managed by a professional. Varies based on the fund's investment strategy (e.g., equity, bond, balanced funds). Mutual funds offer diversification but come with management fees.

4. Exchange-Traded Funds (ETFs): Similar to mutual funds but traded on stock exchanges like individual stocks. Comparable to mutual funds

but often with lower fees. ETFs provide flexibility and can be a cost-effective way to diversify.

5. Real Estate: Investment in physical properties (residential, commercial) or real estate investment trusts (REITs). Can offer steady income through rent and potential appreciation in property value. Requires significant capital and management effort. REITs offer a

more liquid and less hands-on approach.

Risk Management and Diversification

1. Asset Allocation: The process of dividing your investment portfolio among different asset categories (stocks, bonds, real estate) based on your risk tolerance, time horizon, and financial goals. Younger investors

might allocate more to stocks for higher growth potential, while those

closer to retirement might favour bonds for stability.

2. Rebalancing: Periodically adjusting your portfolio to maintain your desired asset allocation. If stocks perform well and exceed your target allocation, you might sell some stocks and buy bonds to restore balance.

3. Dollar-Cost Averaging: Investing a fixed amount of money at regular intervals, regardless of market

conditions. This approach can reduce the impact of market volatility and lower the average cost of your investments over time.

Getting Started with Investing

1. Educate Yourself: Read books, attend workshops, follow financial news, and take online courses to build

your investment knowledge. Seek advice from experienced investors or financial advisors.

2. Start Small: Begin with a small portion of your savings and gradually increase your investments as you become more comfortable. Start with index funds or ETFs to gain exposure to the market with lower risk.

3. Use Investment Apps: Apps like Robinhood, Acorns, and Betterment

can simplify investing and provide tools for beginners. These apps often offer educational resources,

automated investing, and low or no fees.

4. Monitor and Adjust: Regularly review your investments and adjust your strategy as needed to stay aligned with your financial goals. Use portfolio tracking tools and consult with a financial advisor for ongoing guidance.

Chapter 9

Retirement Planning

Planning for retirement early in your career can significantly impact your financial security in later years. The earlier you start, the more time your money has to grow through compound interest.

Determine the lifestyle you want in retirement, including travel, hobbies, and living expenses. Estimate your annual income needs in retirement based on your desired lifestyle and current expenses.

Decide the age at which you plan to retire. This will affect how long your savings need to last. Consider your life expectancy to estimate the duration of your retirement. Use retirement calculators to estimate the total amount you need to save.

Different Retirement Accounts

1. 401(k): Employer-sponsored retirement plan that allows you to contribute a portion of your salary pre-tax. Employers match contributions, tax-deferred growth, and higher contribution limits compared to IRAs. Early withdrawals may incur penalties and taxes. Review investment options within the plan to maximise growth.

2. Individual Retirement Account (IRA): Personal retirement account with tax advantages includes;

-Traditional IRA: Contributions are tax-deductible, and withdrawals are taxed as income in retirement.

- Roth IRA: Contributions are made with after-tax dollars, and qualified withdrawals are tax-free.

Benefits / Consideration: Flexibility in investment choices and tax advantages. Contribution limits and income restrictions apply. Withdrawals before age 59½ may incur penalties.

3. Other Retirement Accounts:

- SEP IRA: Simplified Employee Pension plan for self-employed individuals and small business owners.

- SIMPLE IRA: Savings Incentive Match Plan for Employees, suitable for small businesses.

Strategies for Building a
Retirement Fund

1. Maximise Employer Contributions: Contribute enough to your 401(k) to receive the full employer match. This is essentially free money and can significantly boost your retirement savings.

2. Increase Contributions Over Time: Gradually increase your retirement contributions as your income grows.

Aim to contribute at least 15% of your income towards retirement.

3. Take Advantage of Catch-Up Contributions: If you're 50 or older, utilise catch-up contributions to boost your retirement savings. This allows you to contribute more than the standard limit.

4. Diversify Your Investments: Spread your retirement investments

across various asset classes to reduce risk and enhance growth potential.

5. Monitor and Adjust Your Plan: Regularly review your retirement accounts and adjust your investment strategy as needed. Consult with a financial advisor to ensure you're on track to meet your goals.

Addressing Common Retirement Planning Challenges

Retirement planning can be both exciting and daunting, especially with the myriad of challenges that can arise. From navigating volatile markets to estimating future expenses accurately, here are key strategies to overcome common retirement planning hurdles:

1. Market Volatility: Diversify your investments across asset classes to mitigate risk. Consider a mix of stocks, bonds, and other assets

aligned with your risk tolerance and timeline.

2. Longevity Risk: Plan for a longer lifespan than expected to avoid outliving your savings. Factor in healthcare costs and inflation to ensure your nest egg lasts.

3. Insufficient Savings: Start saving early and consistently. Take advantage of employer-sponsored retirement plans like 401(k)s and

IRAs, and maximise contributions whenever possible.

4. Uncertain Expenses: Estimate your retirement expenses realistically. Include healthcare, housing, and leisure activities. Adjust your budget periodically to reflect changing circumstances.

5. Lack of Knowledge: Educate yourself about retirement planning options. Consult financial advisors or

use online resources to stay informed about investment strategies and retirement products.

By addressing these challenges proactively, you can build a robust retirement plan that provides financial security and peace of mind for your golden years.

Chapter 10

Real Estate and Home Ownership

Owning a home is a significant milestone for many individuals and families, representing not just a financial investment but also a place of stability and personal expression. In this chapter, we explore the various aspects of real estate and home ownership, from the benefits to the considerations and responsibilities involved.

Owning a home offers several advantages that go beyond mere shelter:

1. Building Equity: Unlike renting, where monthly payments go to a landlord, mortgage payments contribute to building equity in your property. Over time, this equity can

be tapped into for future investments or financial needs.

2. Stability and Control: Home ownership provides stability, allowing you to settle into a neighbourhood and community for the long term. You have the freedom to modify and personalise your living space according to your preferences.

3. Potential Tax Benefits:
Homeowners may benefit from tax
deductions on mortgage interest
payments and property taxes, which
can reduce overall tax liabilities.

4. Long-Term Financial Security:
Real estate historically appreciates
over time, offering potential long-
term wealth accumulation. It can
serve as a cornerstone of your

financial portfolio and retirement planning.

Before committing to home ownership, consider these factors:

1. Financial Readiness: Assess your financial situation, including credit score, savings for a down payment,

and ability to afford ongoing expenses like mortgage payments, property taxes, and maintenance costs.

2. Location and Neighborhood: Research the location and neighbourhood where you plan to buy. Consider proximity to amenities, schools (if applicable), safety, and potential for future property value appreciation.

3. Home Type and Size: Determine your housing needs based on family size, lifestyle preferences, and future plans. Decide between single-family homes, condominiums, townhouses, or other types of properties that fit your lifestyle and budget.

4. Long-Term Goals: Consider how buying a home aligns with your long-term goals, such as career plans, family expansion, or retirement

aspirations. Ensure the property suits your anticipated lifestyle changes.

Responsibilities of Home Ownership

Owning a home comes with various responsibilities:

1. Financial Management: Stay on top of mortgage payments, property taxes, homeowners insurance, and

maintenance costs. Budget for unexpected repairs and renovations.

2. Maintenance and Upkeep: Regularly maintain your home to preserve its value and functionality. This includes tasks like landscaping,

HVAC system maintenance, and occasional renovations.

3. Compliance with Local Regulations:Understand and comply

with local zoning laws, building codes, and homeowner association (HOA) rules if applicable. These

regulations may impact property modifications and use.

4. Community Engagement: Participate in community activities and neighbourhood initiatives to

foster a sense of belonging and contribute positively to your surroundings.

Real estate and home ownership represent more than a financial

Transaction; they embody personal aspirations and stability. By carefully considering the benefits, factors, and responsibilities involved, you can make informed decisions that align with your lifestyle and long-term goals.

Chapter 11

Insurance Essentials

Insurance provides financial protection against unexpected events that could otherwise lead to significant financial loss. Understanding different types of insurance and how they work can help you safeguard your financial well-being.

Types of Insurance Coverage

1. Health Insurance: Covers medical expenses, including doctor visits, hospitalisation, prescription medications, and preventive care. Options are; Employer-provided health insurance, individual health plans, or government-sponsored programs like Medicare and Medicaid.

2. Life Insurance: Provides financial support to your beneficiaries (e.g., family members) in the event of your

death. Term life insurance offers coverage for a specific period (e.g., 10, 20 years), while whole life insurance provides lifelong coverage with an investment component. Determine coverage amount based on your financial obligations (e.g., mortgage, education costs) and consider your family's long-term financial needs.

3. Auto Insurance: Covers damages and liability in case of accidents involving your vehicle. Includes

liability coverage (bodily injury and property damage), collision coverage (vehicle repairs), and comprehensive coverage (theft, vandalism, natural disasters). Compare quotes from multiple insurers, review coverage limits and deductibles, and consider additional coverage options (e.g., uninsured motorist coverage).

4. Homeowners/Renters Insurance: Protects your home (structure) and personal belongings (furniture, electronics) against damage or loss

from perils like fire, theft, and natural disasters. Dwelling coverage, personal property coverage, liability protection, and additional living expenses coverage (if you need to live elsewhere temporarily due to damage). Assess your property value, review policy exclusions and limits, and consider adding endorsements for valuable items or specific risks (e.g., flood insurance if you live in a flood-prone area).

Assessing Insurance Needs

Understanding your insurance needs is crucial for safeguarding your financial well-being against unexpected events. Here are key steps to assess your insurance needs effectively:

1. Evaluate Current Coverage:
Review existing insurance policies,
including health, life, auto, home, and
disability insurance. Assess coverage
limits, deductibles, and exclusions to
identify gaps or overlaps in
protection.

2. Identify Risks: Identify potential
risks specific to your life stage,
occupation, and lifestyle. Consider
factors like age, health status,

dependents, income level, and debt obligations.

3. Calculate Financial Obligations: Estimate future financial obligations such as mortgage payments, education costs for children, and retirement expenses. Determine the amount of coverage needed to meet

these obligations in case of unforeseen events.

4. Consider Income Protection: Evaluate the need for income replacement in case of disability or loss of income due to illness, injury, or death. Life insurance and disability income insurance can provide financial support for your family during difficult times.

5. Review Policy Options: Research different insurance policies and

providers to find coverage options that match your needs and budget.

Compare premiums, benefits, and customer reviews to make informed decisions.

6. Consult with an Insurance Professional: Seek advice from an insurance agent or financial advisor who can provide personalised recommendations based on your specific circumstances and risk tolerance.

Managing Insurance Costs

Managing insurance costs is crucial for financial stability and peace of mind. Here are some key strategies to consider:

1. Assess Your Needs Regularly: Review your insurance coverage annually to ensure it aligns with your current life stage and financial situation.

2. Bundle Policies: Consolidate multiple insurance policies (like

home and auto) with one insurer to potentially qualify for discounts.

3. Increase Deductibles: Opt for higher deductibles on your policies to lower monthly premiums, but ensure you can cover the deductible if needed.

4. Maintain a Good Credit Score: Many insurers use credit scores to determine premiums, so improving your credit score can lead to lower insurance costs.

5. Shop Around: Compare quotes from multiple insurers to find the best coverage at the most competitive rates.

6. Take Advantage of Discounts: Inquire about available discounts such as for bundling policies, safe driving records, or home security systems.

7. Consider Term Life Insurance: For life insurance, consider term policies

which offer coverage for a specific period at lower premiums compared to whole life policies.

8. Review Coverage Limits: Ensure your coverage limits are adequate without being excessive, as over-insuring can lead to unnecessary costs.

9. Maintain a Healthy Lifestyle:
Health and life insurance premiums
can often be reduced by maintaining a

healthy lifestyle and quitting
smoking.

10. Ask About Flexible Payment
Options: Inquire if your insurer offers
discounts for paying annually or bi-
annually instead of monthly.

Chapter 12

Philanthropy and Giving Back

Philanthropy involves charitable giving and supporting causes that align with your values and priorities. Incorporating philanthropy into your financial plan allows you to make a positive impact on society and leave a lasting legacy.

Benefits of Charitable Giving

Charitable giving not only benefits the recipients but also brings numerous advantages to the donors and society as a whole:

1. Personal Fulfilment: Giving to charity provides a sense of purpose and satisfaction, knowing that you are making a positive impact on others' lives.

2. Tax Deductions: Donations to eligible charitable organisations can often be deducted from taxable income, reducing your overall tax burden.

3. Community Impact: Charitable donations support essential community services, such as education, healthcare, and social welfare, contributing to societal well-being.

4. Social Responsibility: By giving back, individuals and businesses demonstrate their commitment to social responsibility, which can enhance their reputation and goodwill.

5. Networking and Connections: Involvement in charitable activities can broaden your social network and

connect you with like-minded individuals and organisations.

6. Encouraging Others: Leading by example encourages others to contribute to charitable causes, creating a ripple effect of positive change.

7. Health Benefits: Research suggests that altruistic behaviour, such as charitable giving, can lead to

improved mental and physical health outcomes.

8. Legacy and Impact: Charitable giving allows you to leave a lasting

legacy, supporting causes that are meaningful to you and making a lasting impact on future generations.

9. Philanthropic Growth: Engaging in philanthropy fosters a deeper understanding of societal issues and

encourages ongoing support for important causes.

10. Global Impact: Through international charities and organisations, donors can contribute to global initiatives, addressing

challenges beyond their local community.

Engaging in Impactful Giving

Giving back to society through charitable donations can be a powerful way to make a difference in the world. Whether you're donating money, time, or resources, the key to impactful giving lies in thoughtful consideration and strategic planning. 1. Identify Your Passion: Start by identifying causes that resonate with you personally. Whether it's

education, healthcare, environmental conservation, or social justice, choosing a cause you're passionate about ensures your contributions are meaningful to you.

2. Research and Due Diligence: Once you've identified a cause, research reputable organisations and projects that align with your values and goals. Look for transparency, accountability, and evidence of effectiveness in their programs.

3. Assess Impact: Evaluate how your donations or efforts will create tangible outcomes. Consider metrics such as lives impacted, communities

served, or environmental benefits achieved. Understanding the potential impact allows you to maximise the effectiveness of your giving.

4. Regular Evaluation and Adaptation: Impactful giving is an ongoing process. Regularly evaluate the impact of your contributions and be willing to adapt your approach

based on feedback and changing needs.

5. Collaboration and Amplification: Consider collaborating with others to amplify your impact. Joining forces with like-minded individuals or organisations can leverage resources and expertise for greater collective benefit.

6. Spread Awareness: Share your experiences and encourage others to engage in impactful giving. Raising

awareness about important causes can inspire others to take action and contribute to positive change.

By engaging in thoughtful and impactful giving, you not only contribute to meaningful causes but also become an agent of change in creating a better world for everyone.

Conclusion

Congratulations on completing your journey through "Financial Freedom for Women: Your Ultimate Guide to Money Management and Independence." This book has been crafted with the purpose of empowering you to take control of your financial destiny, equipped with knowledge, confidence, and practical tools to achieve lasting financial independence.

Throughout these pages, you've explored fundamental principles of financial literacy, from budgeting and saving to investing and retirement planning. You've learned how to navigate challenges such as debt management, credit improvement, and career transitions with resilience and foresight. Each chapter has offered insights and strategies tailored to your unique goals and aspirations.

Financial independence is not just about reaching a specific monetary

milestone; it's about gaining the freedom to live life on your terms. It's about having the confidence to pursue your passions, support your loved ones, and make a meaningful impact in your community. As you continue on your journey, remember that financial independence is a continuous process of learning, adapting, and growing.

Your Next Steps

As you close this chapter and embark on the next phase of your financial

journey, remember these key takeaways:
- Set Clear Goals: Define your financial goals and create a roadmap to achieve them. Whether it's saving for retirement, starting a business, or

funding a passion project, clarity of purpose will guide your decisions.

- Stay Informed: Stay abreast of financial trends, investment opportunities, and changes in economic landscapes. Knowledge is

power when it comes to managing your finances effectively.

- Seek Support: Surround yourself with mentors, financial advisors, and a supportive community of women who share your goals and values. Collaboration and shared experiences can accelerate your path to success.

Now is the time to take action. Implement the strategies you've

learned, adapt them to your unique circumstances, and celebrate every milestones along the way. Remember, financial independence is not a destination but a journey of empowerment and self-discovery.

Thank You

Thank you for embarking on this journey with me. It has been an honour to share my knowledge, experiences, and insights with you. As you move forward, may you continue to thrive, inspire others, and embrace the limitless possibilities that financial independence affords.

www.ingramcontent.com/pod-product-compliance
Lightning Source LLC
Chambersburg PA
CBHW071929210526
45479CB00002B/606